WORKSHOP

CH00409074

ROCK BASS LINES

Joe Santerre

Berklee Press

Director: Dave Kusek
Managing Editor: Debbie Cavalier
Marketing Manager: Ola Frank
Sr. Writer/Editor: Jonathan Feist
Writer/Editor: Susan Gedutis
Product Manager: Ilene Altman

ISBN 0-634-01432-3

1140 Boylston Street
Boston, MA 02215-3693 USA
(617) 747-2146

Visit Berklee Press Online at
www.berkleepress.com

DISTRIBUTED BY

HAL•LEONARD®
CORPORATION
7777 W. BLUEMOUND RD. P.O. BOX 13819
MILWAUKEE, WISCONSIN 53213

Visit Hal Leonard Online at
www.halleonard.com

CONTENTS

INTRODUCTION

Welcome to *Rock Bass Lines*. This book is designed to get aspiring bass players started in the art of creating a solid rock bass groove. The examples throughout the book will help you understand how to create a good bass line.

The Basics

Students using this book should know:
- basic music theory;
- the notes on the neck of the bass;
- how to mute open strings so that the only note heard is the one being played.

"Theory Review" pages are provided as a resource for items the student may need to look up while going through the exercises.

The Role of the Bass Player

In any style, the bass's role in the groove is the same: to keep time, and to outline the tonality. When developing bass lines, these two things should always be your goal.

About the Book

There are nine lessons in *Rock Bass Lines*. Each lesson contains several practice exercises, a rock song that utilizes the exercises, and play-along tracks on the accompanying CD. Also included in each lesson is a section for you to write out your own bass grooves.

In addition to the exercises and play along opportunities in this book, you can learn a lot by listening to bass players on recordings and trying to imitate what they are playing. There is a suggested listening list at the beginning of every lesson.

Before you get started, make sure:
- your bass is in tune;
- you're consistent with your attacks for each note;
- you play with some attitude!

About the CD

The examples on the CD are played four times: twice with drums, guitar, and my original bass lines, and twice with drums and guitar, but without my bass lines, so that you can play along and experiment creating your own rock bass grooves. The songs are played twice: once with the bass and once without.

The songs and examples in this book correspond to the tracks on the CD; example 14 in the book is track 14 on the CD. Each track starts with a one-measure count-off ($\frac{4}{4}$ has four clicks, $\frac{12}{8}$ has twelve). Try to become familiar with the notes and rhythms in each example before playing along with the CD.

At the end of the accompanying CD, there is a track from my own recording, *The Scenic Route,* and a track from the Jon Finn Group's CD, *Wicked*. Pay close attention to the bass lines in these songs. These cuts illustrate many of the concepts taught throughout the book.

How to Use this Book

Remember, your goal is to be able to create your own bass grooves. Be comprehensive in your approach.

1. Practice these examples thoroughly, and concentrate on accuracy and feel. To really absorb this material, you should take your time, and be methodical and focused.
2. Listen to the bands and players you admire, and try to figure out their bass lines.
3. Experiment with your own creations. If you already play in a band, create your own bass lines using this book's examples as models.

Good luck and have fun!

—Joe Santerre

THEORY REVIEW

Before you start lesson 1, you should understand the following topics.

Notation

Notes are written on a *staff*.

Bass music is usually written using the *bass clef* staff. Here are the notes for the lines and spaces in bass clef.

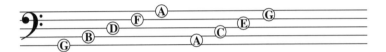

Ledger Lines

The staff can be extended with *ledger lines*.

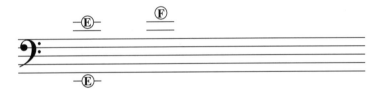

Accidentals

Accidentals before notes raise or lower the pitch.

♭   *Flat:* next note down (half step, or one fret down)

♯   *Sharp:* next note up (half step up, or one fret up)

♮   *Natural*: cancels a flat or sharp

Key Signatures

To indicate a tune's key, and to show which notes always get sharps or flats, use a key signature. Accidentals on the lines and spaces in the key signature affect those notes unless there is a natural sign.

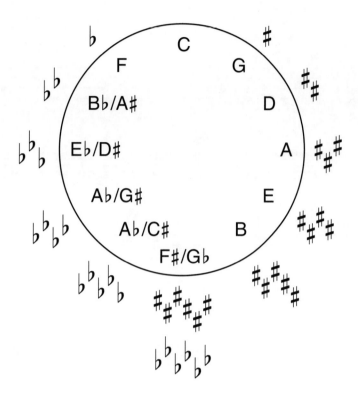

The following key signature, D, indicates that all F and C notes in the music will become F-sharps and C-sharps.

Notice there are no Cs in the previous example. It is common to have a key signature specify a sharped note, even though it may not appear in the music.

Rhythms

These are the basic rhythms.

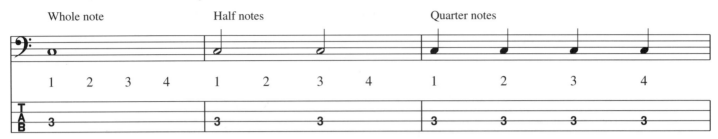

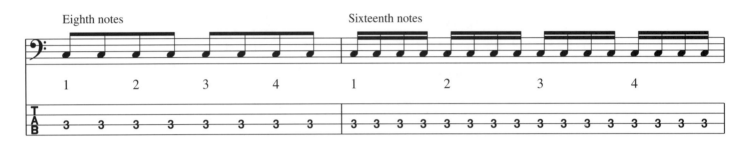

Connect notes using a *tie*.

Extend a note's rhythmic value by using a *dot*. A dot increases the value by one half.

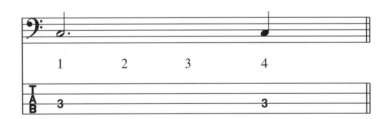

Triplets squeeze three even attacks (in this case, eighth notes) into the space of two attacks (two eighth notes, or one quarter-note beat).

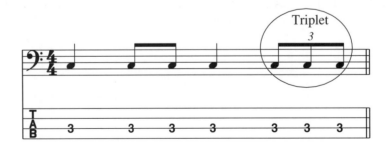

Measures and Time Signatures

Groups of beats are divided into *measures*. Measure lengths are shown with *time signatures*. This measure is in $\frac{4}{4}$ time—there are four quarter notes in the measure.

A "C" stands for *common time,* and it means the same thing as $\frac{4}{4}$ time.

In $\frac{12}{8}$ time, there are twelve eighth notes per measure.

Scales

To be a rock bassist, you should know the following types of scales. Practice them in all keys, two octaves. Also, to become more familiar with the fretboard, practice them in different positions.

Major Scale: C Major

Dorian Scale: C Dorian

Natural Minor Scale: C Natural Minor

Harmonic Minor Scale: C Harmonic Minor

Mixolydian Scale: C Mixolydian

Minor-Pentatonic Scale

The *minor-pentatonic scale* will be used for a large percentage of your rock bass playing. This scale consists of the root, minor third, fourth, fifth, and the minor seventh scale degrees. The following example is the G minor pentatonic scale.

G Minor Pentatonic Scale

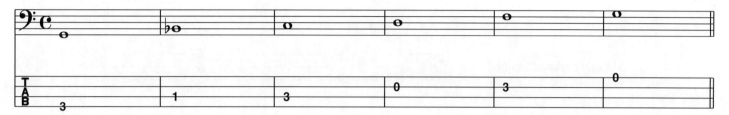

Major Pentatonic Scale

The *major pentatonic scale* will also be used for a large percentage of your rock bass playing. This scale consists of the root, second, third, fifth, and sixth scale degrees. The following example is the Bb major pentatonic scale. Note: the Bb major pentatonic scale uses the same notes as the G minor pentatonic scale!

Bb Major Pentatonic Scale

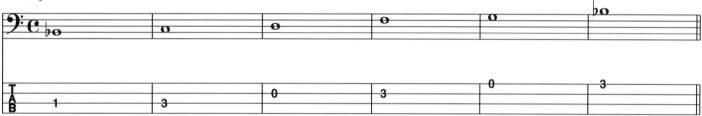

Blues Scale

The *blues scale* is also very common in rock bass line construction. It is made up of the same notes as the minor pentatonic scale with the addition of the flatted fifth scale degree. The following example is the G blues scale.

G Blues Scale

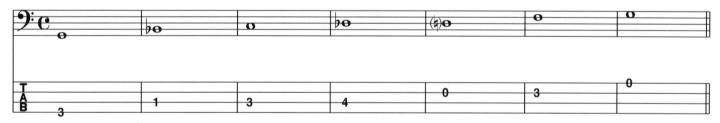

There are scale exercises in the back of the book for the minor pentatonic, major pentatonic, and blues scales.

Chords

A *chord* is made when three or more notes are sounded simultaneously. Often chords are made up of the root, third, fifth, and seventh scale degrees. Below are several chords commonly used in rock styles.

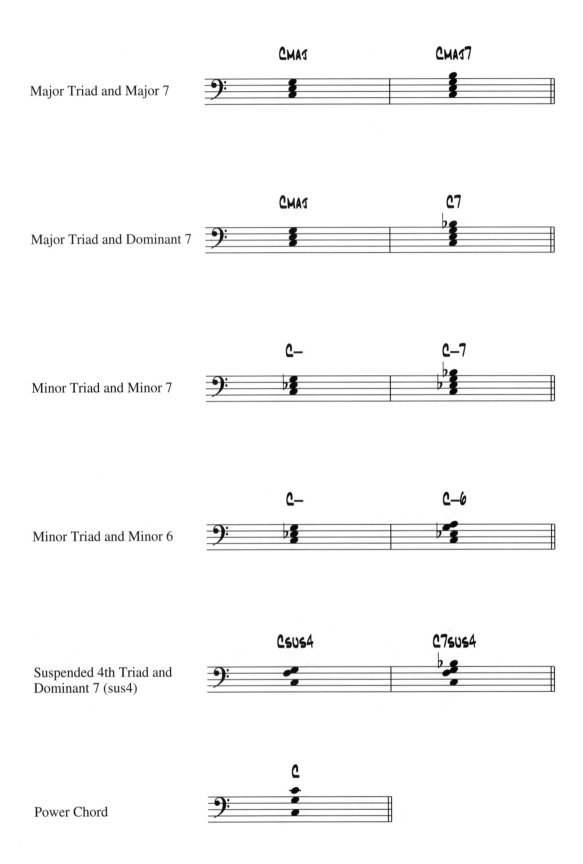

Arpeggios

Bass players usually play chords as arpeggios. An *arpeggio* is a series of chord tones played one at a time. They usually contain the root, third, fifth, and seventh scale degrees. The following arpeggios are used commonly in rock bass playing.

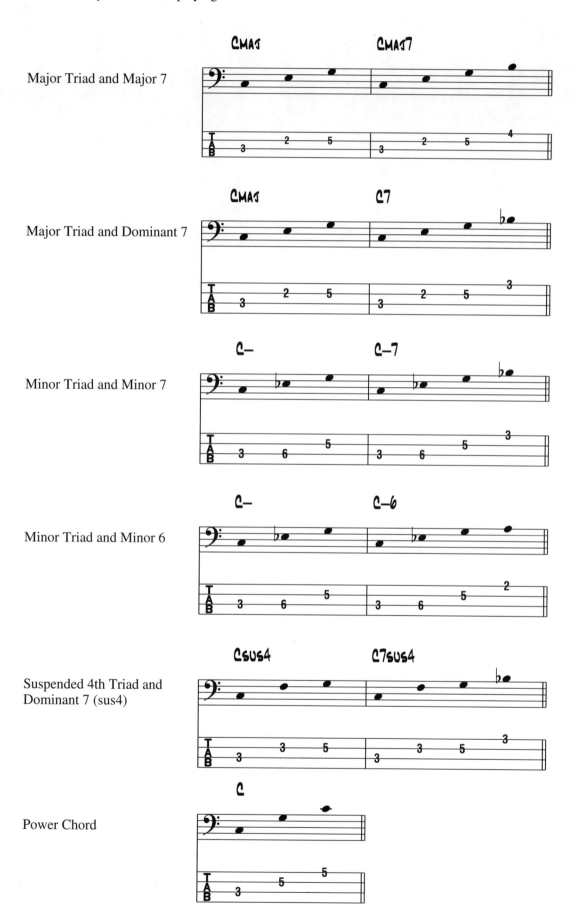

LESSON 1: ONE-CHORD ROCK

Many rock bass lines are based on just one chord. Each example in this lesson will use only the root, fifth, and the octave of the chord. For more examples of this type of bass playing, listen to bands like Led Zeppelin, the James Gang, and Deep Purple.

1 **Example 1**

Tuning Notes: E–A–D–G strings, played twice.

2 **Example 2**

3 **Example 3**

4 **Example 4**

5 **Example 5**

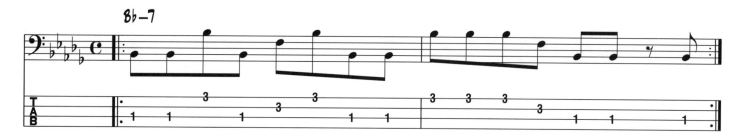

lesson 1
one-chord rock

The following examples provide more experience playing bass lines over one chord. Be careful with the tied notes in example 8 and the rhythm in example 9.

6 **Example 6**

7 **Example 7**

8 **Example 8**

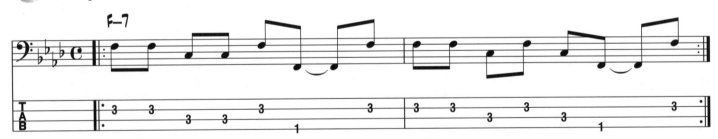

9 **Example 9**

WRITE YOUR OWN

In the following blank measures, write your own bass grooves for the chord indicated. Remember, the goal is to outline the chord; start with the root, fifth, and octave. Model your own rhythms after those used in the examples.

1.

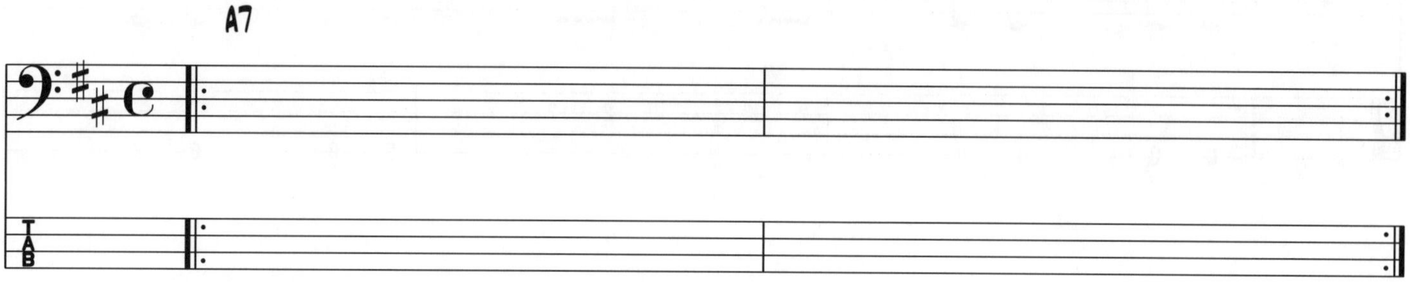

A7

2.

F#(NO3)

3.

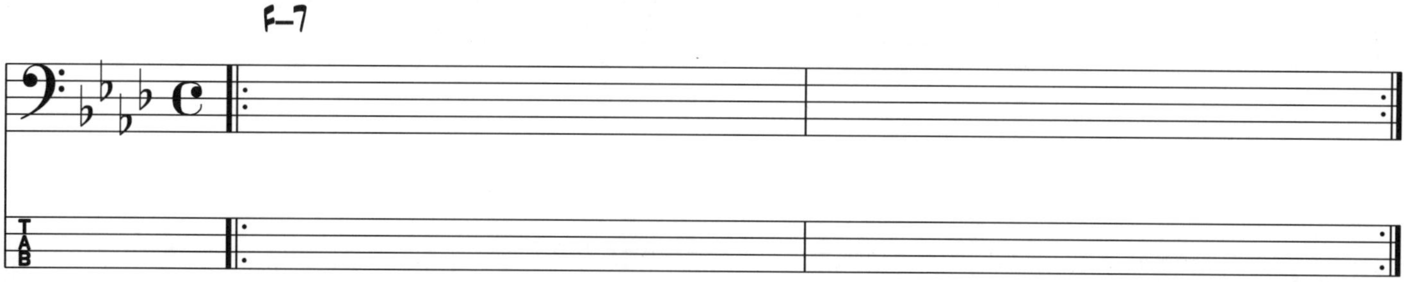

F—7

4.

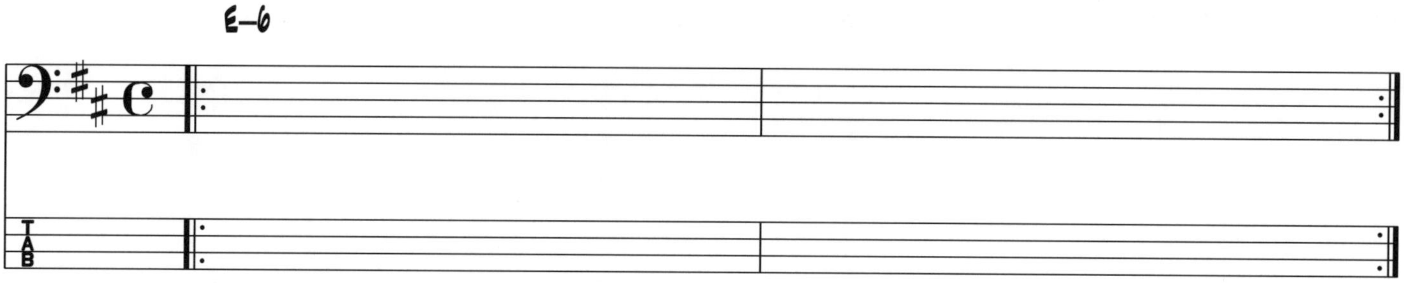

E—6

10 Song 1

HEAVY BALLOON

LESSON 2: TWO-CHORD ROCK

This lesson focuses on progressions with two chords in a phrase. Sometimes, in addition to the root, fifth and octave, the third and seventh of the chord will be used in the bass line. Chances are that some of the rock grooves you may be asked to create will be over a progression with two chord changes. For more examples of this type of bass playing, listen to bands like the Red Hot Chili Peppers, the Cars, and Sting.

11 Example 11

12 Example 12

13 Example 13

14 Example 14

Here are a few more bass lines based on two chords. Practice these examples alone and then with the bass and drum tracks. When you feel comfortable with these examples, try to play along with the tracks that have no bass. Then create your own bass line.

15 **Example 15**

16 **Example 16**

17 **Example 17**

18 **Example 18**

These examples still have two chords, but now each chord is two measures long.

19 Example 19

20 Example 20

lesson 2
two-chord rock

21 Example 21

WRITE YOUR OWN

Create bass grooves for the following two-chord exercises, then write them down. Remember, the line you create should outline the chord. Model your own rhythms after those used in the examples.

1.

F   Bb

2.

A–   D–

3.

C   F#

4.

E–6   E–6

C7   C7

22 Song 2

CURRIED CHICKEN

Here's a song that combines examples 14 and 20. This song is similar to something the Red Hot Chili Peppers would play. Practice with the CD. There are two main sections in this song: A and B.

LESSON 3: MULTIPLE CHORDS

In this chapter, we'll explore rock bass lines with more than two chords. Notice that the following examples all use the root of the chord with a defining rhythm. For more examples of this kind of bass playing, listen to bands like Aerosmith, Black Sabbath, and Metallica.

23 Example 23

24 Example 24

11

For examples 25 and 26, be very precise with the rhythms in each measure and the attacks for each note.

25 **Example 25**

In this example, you must have a low B string or a "hip shot" on your E string to play the low notes in parentheses.

26 **Example 26**

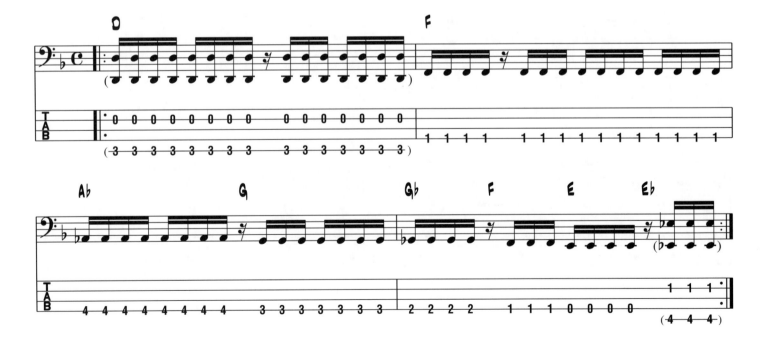

WRITE YOUR OWN

Write in your own bass grooves for the chords indicated below. These chord progressions are the same as examples 23 to 25, so you can practice your original bass lines with the drum tracks. Be sure to follow the harmonic rhythm (the rhythm of each chord progression).

27 Song 3

SOUR VIBE

This song is a twelve-bar blues in the key of A. It uses three chords: A7 (the I chord), D7 (the IV chord), and E7 (the V chord). There are many variations of blues, but two characteristics of almost all blues progressions are the IV chord in the fifth measure and the V chord in the ninth measure. "Sour Vibe" is a twelve-bar blues that is played in a style similar to the band Aerosmith.

28 Song 4

BLACK METAL

This song uses a repetitive rhythm with several different chords. It is a heavy metal rock bass groove in the style of Black Sabbath or Metallica.

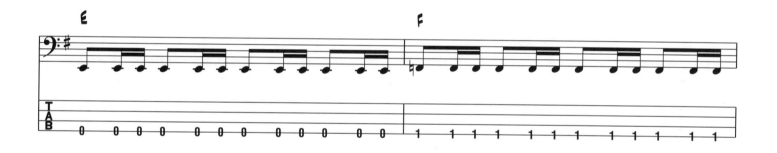

LESSON 4: EIGHTH-NOTE GROOVES

The continuous eighth-note line is a popular rock groove. Although it may appear to be an easy groove to play, there is a lot to it. The idea is to keep the time and intensity as consistent as possible. Keep these two goals in mind while playing the following examples.

A good way to build consistency is through repetition. After practicing with the CD, try playing each example with a metronome, for two minutes at a time. Listen to how each note is attacked. It is helpful to record yourself and then listen to how consistent you are each time you play a phrase. The first time you play a phrase should sound identical to the third, tenth, or even twentieth time.

For more examples of this kind of bass playing, listen to bands like the Police, the Rolling Stones, and the Who.

29 Example 29

30 Example 30

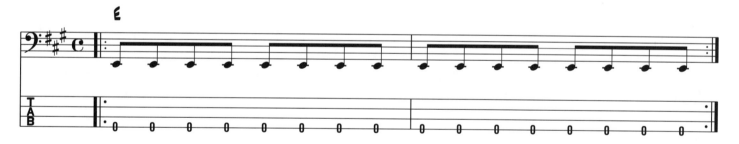

31 Example 31

17

32 Example 32

33 Example 33

In this example, you must have a low B string or a "hip shot" on your E string to play the low notes in parentheses.

34 Example 34

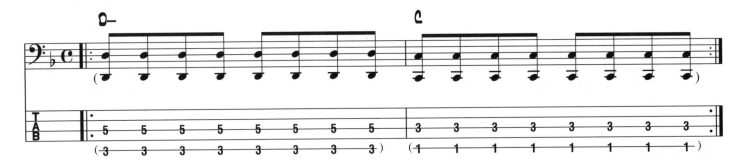

35 Example 35

36 Example 36

37 Example 37

38 Example 38

39 Example 39

WRITE YOUR OWN

Write your own bass grooves for the chords indicated below.

1.

G−

2.

B♭7

3.

E−7   A7

4.

D−6

E−7   E♭7

40 Song 5

GENERICA

In this bass line, the song form follows a twelve-bar blues pattern. This blues is in the key of G. It uses three chords: G7 (the I chord), C7 (the IV chord), and D7 (the V chord). All blues progressions are rooted in this three-chord progression.

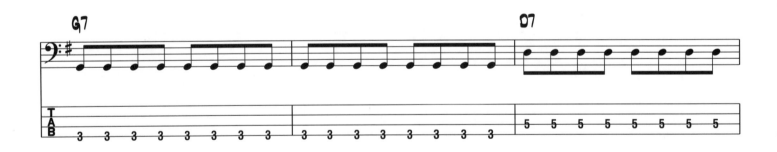

41 Song 6

FIFTEASE

In this blues progression, the line is a variation of the previous example. Notice it is the same chord progression but with more notes of the scale and arpeggio for each chord symbol. This line is used in countless early rock 'n' roll songs. Even today, it still does the job of outlining the chords and keeping time.

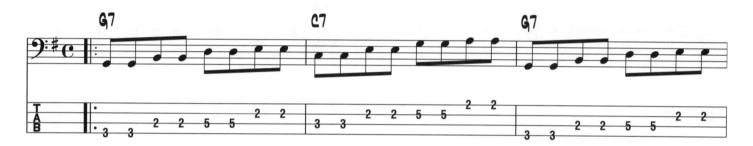

42 Song 7

COPS & ROBBERS

Here's a song using a continual eighth-note bass line in the style of The Police. There are three sections in this song, labeled A, B, and C.

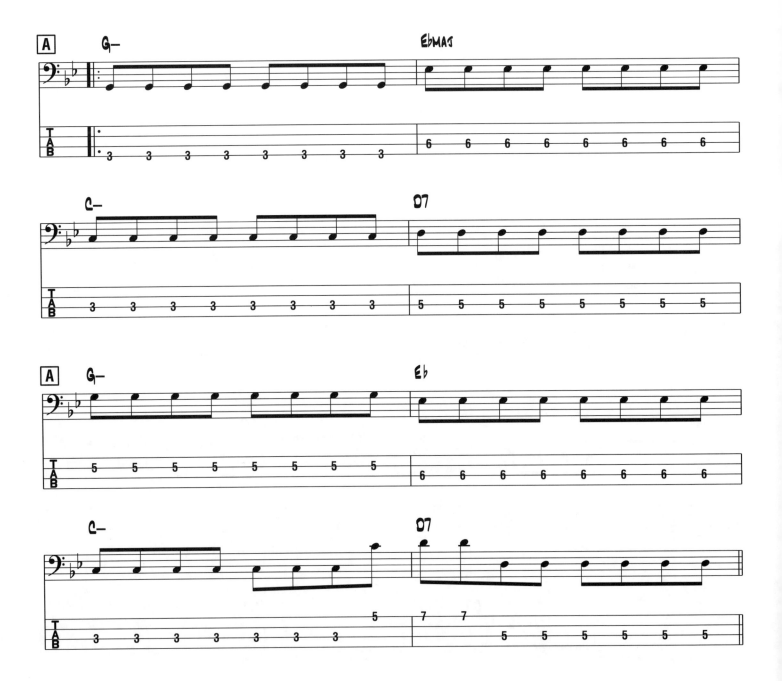

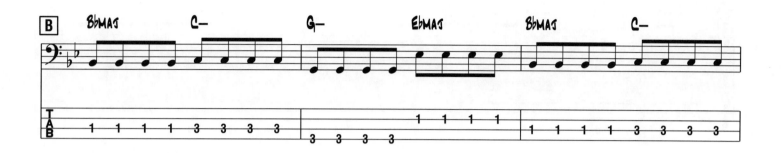

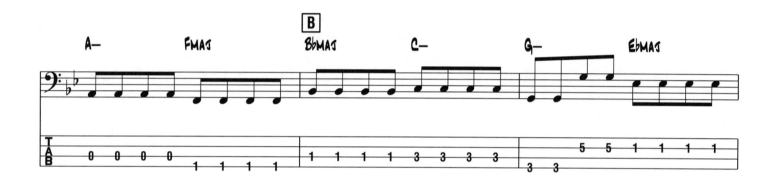

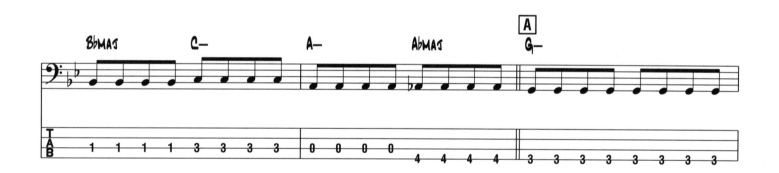

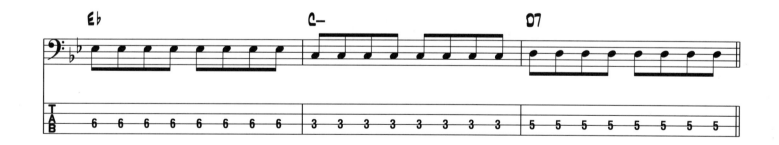

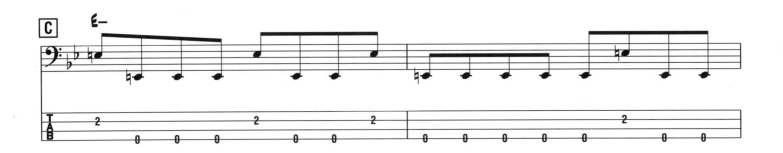

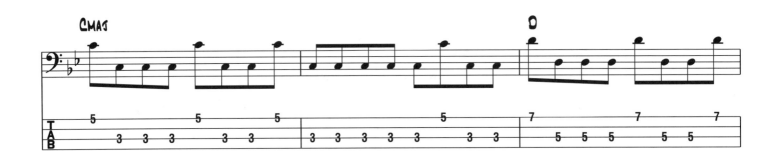

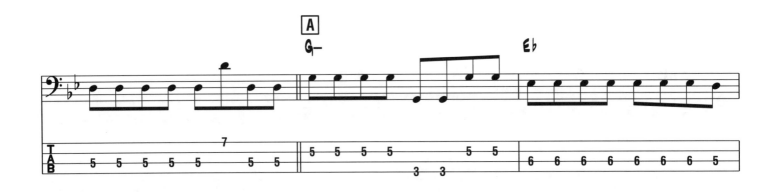

LESSON 5: REVIEW

Each of the following grooves is a variation of the first eight groove exercises in lessons 1 and 2.

43 Example 43

44 Example 44

45 Example 45

46 Example 46

47 Example 47

48 Example 48

49 Example 49

50 Example 50

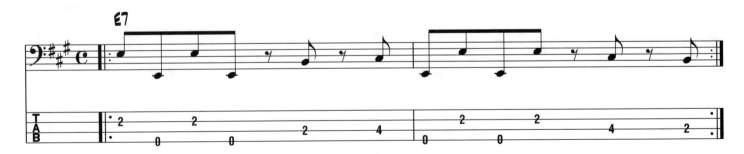

51 Example 51

52 Example 52

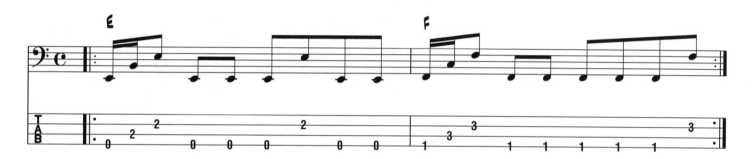

53 Example 53

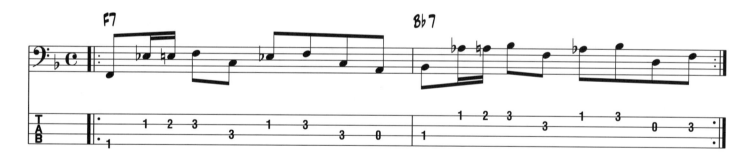

54 Example 54

55 Example 55

56 Example 56

57 Example 57

58 Example 58

LESSON 6: KICK BASS LINES

Kick lines are bass lines that contain short notes and a lot of space, and often double the kick drum. Timing is everything when playing kick bass lines. After you become familiar with the kick bass line examples below, try to match your bass playing with the bass on the recording.

When playing with a band, try to be aware of the other players, and lock in with each other's time. Practicing with the accompanying CD, a metronome, or a drum sequence will help strengthen your inner time feel.

For more examples of this kind of bass playing, listen to bands like Jamiroquai, Dream Theater, and Yes.

59 Example 59

60 Example 60

61 Example 61

62 Example 62

lesson 6
kick bass lines

63 Example 63

64 Example 64

65 Example 65

WRITE YOUR OWN

Use these blank measures to write your own kick bass grooves.

66 Song 8

KICK BOXER

This song uses three different sections of kick bass lines. It is similar in style to Jamiroquai's music. The drum track consists only of the hi-hat. Concentrate on your rhythm and time.

Notice the last measure of this song is blank, with "bass fill" indicated. This simply means to create a bass line to fill that space. You can use the same notes that are used in the bass part. The most important thing is to continue with the written bass part on time.

LESSON 7: LICK GROOVES

In this chapter, there are several examples of "lick" or "concerted" rock bass grooves. This type of bass line is usually doubled with the guitar or keyboard part in an arrangement. Lick groove bass lines often consist of notes from the minor pentatonic or blues scale, but can be based on any tonality. Try to figure out which scale is being used for each example.

For more examples of this kind of bass playing, listen to bands like Steve Morse, The Dixie Dregs, and Kansas.

67 Example 67

68 Example 68

69 Example 69

70 Example 70

71 Example 71

72 Example 72

73 Example 73

74 Example 74

WRITE YOUR OWN

Write some of your own lick bass lines for the chord changes listed below. Try using either the minor pentatonic or blues scale for each lick.

75 Song 9

LICK BOXER

LESSON 8: SHUFFLE—$\frac{12}{8}$

In a shuffle feel, each pulse or beat is divided into three parts. A shuffle, or "12/8 feel" can be counted or felt two different ways.

You can count every eighth note (1 to 12):

Or else, you can count the first note of every eighth-note triplet (1 to 4), making it feel like $\frac{4}{4}$ with a triplet underneath:

They sound the same. Players generally feel more comfortable feeling it one way or the other. Experiment with counting it both ways.

Examples 76 and 77 will help you get used to the pulse of a shuffle. Example 79 is the same as example 78, except that the first two eighths of each beat are tied together. Note that each example on this page is written in $\frac{12}{8}$ time.

For more examples of this kind of bass playing, listen to bands like ZZ Top, James Cotton, and Muddy Waters.

76 Example 76

77 Example 77

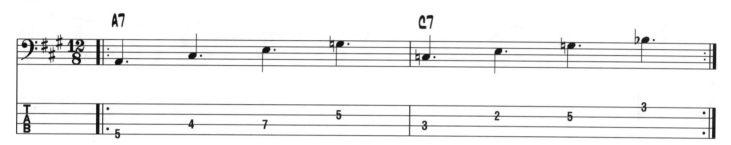

78 Example 78

79 Example 79

80 Example 80

81 Example 81

82 Example 82

WRITE YOUR OWN

Create your own rock shuffle bass lines for the chords indicated below.

1.

A–7

2.

F7

3.

G–7   C7

4.

B♭–7

C–   F7

83 Song 10

YY BOTTOM

This song is a shuffle in that gutsy, rootsy style of ZZ Top.

LESSON 9: ODD-TIME BASS LINES

With odd-time grooves, your primary goal is still to outline the tonality of each chord. The only thing that is a little different, if you haven't played in odd time before, is the timing and pulse.

For more examples of this kind of bass playing, listen to bands like Frank Zappa, Dream Theater, and Yes.

84 **Example 84**

85 **Example 85**

86 **Example 86**

lesson 9
odd-time bass lines

87 Example 87

88 Example 88

89 Example 89

Let each note ring while you attack the next note.

90 Example 90

WRITE YOUR OWN

Create your own odd-time bass lines. Remember to outline the chord, either with arpeggio or scale notes.

1.

E–7

2.

G–7   Bb7

3.

A–7   D7

4.

E–7   A7

G7sus4   F–7

SCALES

MAJOR PENTATONIC SCALE EXERCISES

The following exercises use the major pentatonic scale. Every example contains notes from its respective major pentatonic scale only. Remember that accidentals carry through the measure.

G Major Pentatonic

A Major Pentatonic

F Major Pentatonic

E Major Pentatonic

Ab Major Pentatonic

F# Major Pentatonic

C Major Pentatonic

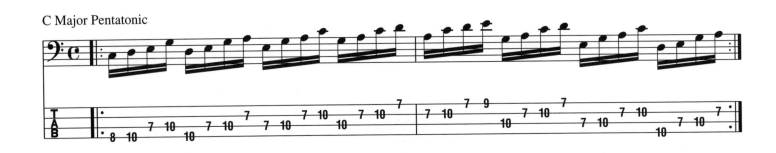

B Major Pentatonic

WRITE YOUR OWN

Create your own major-pentatonic scale exercises. Try mixing different rhythms.

A Major Pentatonic

F# Major Pentatonic

C# Major Pentatonic

D Major Pentatonic

G Major Pentatonic

MINOR PENTATONIC SCALE EXERCISES

The following exercises use the minor pentatonic scale. All of the examples can be played "in position" (four frets). Use these exercises to build your technique, strengthen your time, and become more familiar with scales and the notes on the neck. Every example contains notes from the respective minor pentatonic scale only.

G Minor Pentatonic

A Minor Pentatonic

F Minor Pentatonic

E Minor Pentatonic

G♯ Minor Pentatonic

F♯ Minor Pentatonic

C Minor Pentatonic

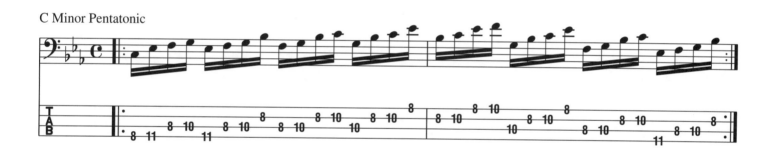

B Minor Pentatonic

WRITE YOUR OWN

Create your own minor pentatonic scale exercises. Try mixing different rhythms.

C Minor Pentatonic

A Minor Pentatonic

E Minor Pentatonic

F Minor Pentatonic

B♭ Minor Pentatonic

BLUES SCALE EXERCISES

The following exercises use the blues scale. All of the examples can be played "in position" (four frets). Remember, the blues scale is the minor pentatonic scale with the addition of one other note: the ♭5 (or ♯4).

Use these exercises to build your technique, strengthen your time, and become more familiar with fingering the blues scales. Every example contains notes from the respective blues scale only.

G Blues Scale

A Blues Scale

B♭ Blues Scale

E Blues Scale

C Blues Scale

F Blues Scale

A Blues Scale

WRITE YOUR OWN

Create your own blues scale exercises. Try mixing different rhythms.

G Blues Scale

A Blues Scale

B♭ Blues Scale

E Blues Scale

C Blues Scale

F Blues Scale

ABOUT THE AUTHOR

JOE SANTERRE

Joe Santerre has performed, taught, and lectured internationally as an expert in rock bass techniques. Among his former students are Brian Beller (Dweezil Zappa, Mike Keneally), Chris Chaney (Alanis Morrissette, Robin Ford), and John DeServio (Vinnie Moore, Lita Ford). Joe has performed with such luminaries as Tom Coster (Vital Information, Santana), John Petrucci (Dream Theatre), Vinnie Moore, Steve Morse (Dixie Dregs, Kansas), Blues Saraceno, Andy Timmons, and many others. He is currently the bassist for the Jon Finn Group with bass credits on *Wicked* and *Don't Look So Serious*. He also writes for *Bass Frontiers* magazine and teaches at Berklee College of Music. His recent solo album, *The Scenic Route*, features his own compositions and arrangements.

Thanks to Jon Finn for guitar performances.

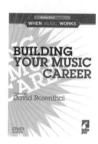

THE BEST OF BERKLEE PRESS

MUSIC BUSINESS

How to Get a Job in the Music & Recording Industry
by Keith Hatschek
0-634-01868-X Book $24.95

Mix Masters: Platinum Engineers Reveal Their Secrets for Success
by Maureen Droney
0-87639-019-X Book $24.95

The Musician's Internet
by Peter Spellman
0-634-03586-X Book $24.95

The New Music Therapist's Handbook, Second Edition
by Suzanne B. Hanser
0-634-00645-2 Book $29.95

The Self-Promoting Musician
by Peter Spellman
0-634-00644-4 Book $24.95

SONGWRITING / ARRANGING / VOICE

Arranging for Large Jazz Ensemble
by Ken Pullig
0-634-03656-4 Book/CD $39.95

Complete Guide to Film Scoring
by Richard Davis
0-634-00636-3 Book $24.95

The Contemporary Singer
By Anne Peckham
0-634-00797-1 Book/CD $24.95

Essential Ear Training
by Steve Prosser
0-634-00640-1 Book $14.95

Jazz Composition: Theory and Practice
By Ted Pease
0-87639-001-7 Book/CD $39.95

Melody in Songwriting
by Jack Perricone
0-634-00638-X Book $19.95

Modern Jazz Voicings
by Ted Pease and Ken Pullig
0-634-01443-9 Book/CD $24.95

Music Notation
by Mark McGrain
0-7935-0847-9 Book $19.95

Reharmonization Techn iques
by Randy Felts
0-634-01585-0 Book $29.95

The Songs of John Lennon
by John Stevens
0-634-01795-0 Book $24.95

The Songwriter's Workshop: Melody
by Jimmy Kachulis
0-634-02659-3 Book $24.95

Songwriting: Essential Guide to Lyric Form & Structure
by Pat Pattison
0-7935-1180-1 Book $14.95

Songwriting: Essential Guide to Rhyming
by Pat Pattison
0-7935-1181-X Book $14.95

BERKLEE PRACTICE METHOD

0-634-00650-9 **Bass** by Rich Appleman and John Repucci
0-634-00652-5 **Drum Set** by Ron Savage and Casey Scheuerell
0-634-00649-5 **Guitar** by Larry Baione
0-634-00651-7 **Keyboard** by Russell Hoffmann and Paul Schmeling
0-634-00795-5 **Alto Sax** by Jim Odgren and Bill Pierce
0-634-00798-0 **Tenor Sax** by Jim Odgren and Bill Pierce
0-634-00791-2 **Trombone** by Jeff Galindo
0-634-00790-4 **Trumpet** by Tiger Okoshi and Charles Lewis
0-634-00794-7 **Vibraphone** by Ed Saindon
0-634-00792-0 **Violin** by Matt Glaser and Mimi Rabson
Book/CD $14.95 (each)

BERKLEE INSTANT SERIES

0-634-01667-9 **Bass** by Danny Morris
0-634-02602-X **Drum Set** by Ron Savage
0-634-02951-7 **Guitar** by Tomo Fujita
0-634-03141-4 **Keyboard** by Paul Schmeling and Dave Limina
Book/CD $14.95 (each)

IMPROVISATION

Blues Improvisation Complete Series
by Jeff Harrington
0-634-01530-3 Bb Instruments
0-634-01532-X C Bass Instruments
0-634-00647-9 C Treble Instruments
0-634-01531-7 Eb Instruments
Book/CD $19.95 (each)

A Guide to Jazz Improvisation Series
by John LaPorta
0-634-00700-9 C Instruments
0-634-00762-9 Bb Instruments
0-634-00763-7 Eb Instruments
0-634-00764-5 Bass Clef
Book $16.95 (each)

MUSIC TECHNOLOGY

Arranging in the Digital World
by Corey Allen
0-634-00634-7 Book/MIDI Disk $19.95

Finale: An Easy Guide to Music Notation
by Tom Rudolph and Vince Leonard
0-634-01666-0 Book/CD-ROM $59.95

Producing in the Home Studio with Pro Tools Second Edition
by David Franz
0-87639-008-4 Book/CD-ROM $34.95

Recording in the Digital World
by Tom Rudolph and Vince Leonard
0-634-01324-6 Book $29.95

POP CULTURE

Inside the Hits
by Wayne Wadhams
0-634-01430-7 Book $29.95

Masters of Music: Conversations with Berklee Greats
by Mark Small and Andrew Taylor
0-634-00642-8 Book $24.95